TYLER M

THE KIDS COMPASS GUIDE

EASY & FUN WAY TO MASTER NAVIGATION SKILLS. COLORFUL ILLUSTRATIONS, QUIZZES, AND 15+ INTERACTIVE GAMES TO ENGAGE KIDS WITH NATURE.

EXCLUSIVE FREE BONUS FOR YOU!

DON'T FORGET TO DOWNLOAD IT

JUMP NOW TO THE END OF THE BOOK

AND SCAN THE QR CODE!

TABLE OF CONTENT

WELCOME ADVENTURER!

Hey there, young explorer! Are you ready for an awesome adventure into the world of compass exploration? This book will help you become a real explorer. As you flip through these pages, you'll master the art of using a compass, hone your navigation skills, and uncover tales of past explorers.

Inside, you'll find simple steps and fun activities to teach you about the magnetic compass. From holding it to reading it, you'll learn to find your way outdoors. Plus, we've included quizzes and games to make learning fun!

The compass is a powerful tool that points you in the right direction. Learning to use it is key for any adventurer, whether in forests or your backyard. Keep reading to unlock the mysteries of the compass and start your adventure!

WHY USE A COMPASS?

Knowing how to use a compass is super important and awesome! Imagine you're trekking through the woods, camping with your family, or exploring on a school trip. A compass can be your best buddy, ensuring you never lose your way.

Using a compass isn't just fun—it's also about being smart and self-reliant. Whether you're out exploring without a map

or your GPS stops working, your trusty compass will always be there to point you in the right direction. If you're hiking and need to find your way back to the trail, your compass will show you. Or if you're off on a camping adventure and want to roam around, your compass will lead you right back to your cozy campsite.

But wait, there's more!

A compass isn't just a tool—it's a key to learning and excitement. It teaches you directions and helps you understand the world. By mastering the compass, you're not just ready for outdoor adventures, but you're also gaining a skill that keeps you safe and confident!

CHAPTER 1
THE STORY OF THE COMPASS

The tale of the compass is a mesmerizing journey through time! This incredible tool has been guiding adventurers for thousands of years, starting way back in ancient China. Around 2000 years ago, the clever folks there stumbled upon a magical stone called lodestone. They realized that when this special stone was set afloat on water, it had a knack for pointing towards the North. And just like that, the very first seeds of the compass were planted!

Fast forward to the 11th century, and the Chinese had crafted the very first magnetic compasses for sea navigation.

These early compasses were simple yet ingenious—just a lodestone or magnetized needle resting on a piece of wood and bobbing in water. With this handy device, sailors could find their way even on cloudy days or pitch-black nights, making their long journeys much safer and smoother.

As time passed, the compass reached Europe and the Mediterranean by the 12th century. It became essential for sailors, guiding explorers like Columbus and Marco Polo to new horizons. With the compass, they charted unknown waters and discovered new lands, changing history forever.

But the compass didn't stop there! Over the years, it evolved into more sophisticated forms, like the dry compass with its pivoting needle and the modern magnetic compass with its spinning dial. These upgrades made the compass even more precise and user-friendly, cementing its status as a true marvel of invention.

The compass isn't just for navigation—it's a game-changer that reshaped the world. It enabled adventurers to explore new frontiers, boosted trade routes, and expanded our understanding of the world.

So, the next time you hold a compass in your hands, remember: it's not just a tool—it's a symbol of endless possibilities, waiting to lead you on your own thrilling adventures!

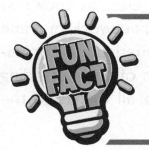

Did you know that early Chinese compasses were often shaped like a spoon? The handle of the spoon would point south, helping travelers and sailors find their way long before the modern compass was invented!

FAMOUS EXPLORERS AND HOW THEY USED THE COMPASS

The history of exploration is brimming with tales of intrepid adventurers who relied on the compass to chart their extraordinary voyages. One such luminary is **Christopher Columbus.** In 1492, Columbus embarked on a daring expedition from Spain in search of a new route to Asia. Armed with a trusty magnetic compass, Columbus and his crew navigated the vast expanse of the Atlantic Ocean. The com-

pass proved indispensable in steering them on course, ultimately leading to the epochal discovery of the Americas. Without the compass as their faithful guide, Columbus may never have set foot on the shores of the New World!

Another luminary whose odyssey was guided by the compass is **Marco Polo.** In the 13th century, Polo embarked on an epic odyssey from Italy to China—a monumental journey spanning over two decades. The compass was an invaluable ally to Polo and his fellow travelers as they traversed the legendary Silk Road, a historic network of trade routes bridging the East and West. Polo's meticulous chronicles of his travels illuminated a new realm of understanding and commerce between Europe and Asia, all thanks to the compass's unwavering guidance.

Ferdinand Magellan, a Portuguese explorer, also owed much to the compass during his historic circumnavigation of the globe in the early 16th century. Magellan's groundbreaking voyage marked the first successful circumnavigation of the Earth, affirming the planet's spherical shape and interconnected oceans. The compass served as an indispensable tool for navigating uncharted waters and ensuring the crew's safe passage through perilous seas.

The compass was more than a navigational tool; it sparked a new era of exploration, transforming long-distance maritime travel and expanding knowledge and trade. With the compass, explorers reshaped history and broadened our understanding of the world.

So, when you use a compass, you're following in the footsteps of great explorers like Columbus, Marco Polo, and Magellan. Use it to embark on thrilling journeys and make amazing discoveries!

CHAPTER 2

THE ABC'S OF COMPASSES

Before we dive into using a compass, it's important to build a strong foundation—just like starting a house from the ground up. In this chapter, you'll learn all the essential information that will help you use a compass skillfully and confidently. First, let's uncover what lies behind the simple, yet fascinating tool that always points north with such ease.

So get ready to dive into the marvelous world of compasses and start your journey of mastering this incredible tool!

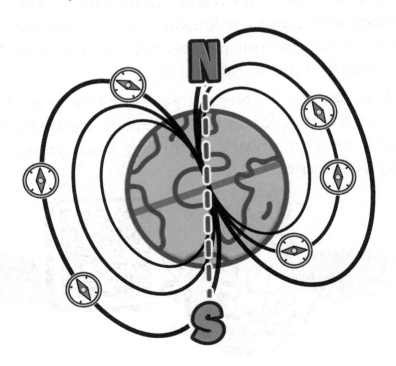

WHY A COMPASS POINTS NORTH

Have you ever wondered why every compass needle always points north? It might seem like magic, but it's actually all thanks to Earth's magnetism!

Believe it or not, our Earth is a giant magnet! This is because of Earth's outer core, which is made up of molten iron and other metals. As Earth spins, these liquid metals move around, and this movement creates what we call a magnetic field.

The movement of molten iron and other metals in the outer core generates electric currents. These currents create magnetic fields, and when added up, they give Earth a magnetic field strong enough to influence the compass needle. This phenomenon is known as the dynamo effect.

The needle of a compass is lightweight and can spin freely. One end, usually painted red, is magnetized and always points to the magnetic north pole. This magnetic north pole is located in the Arctic regions of Canada and moves slightly over time due to changes in Earth's magnetic field.

Just like fridge magnets pull towards metal objects, Earth's magnetic field has a north and south pole that attract magnetic things.

So, when you hold a compass and see the needle point north, you're witnessing Earth's magnetic field at work! This amazing natural phenomenon helps you navigate and explore the world like the great adventurers before you. Isn't it fascinating how our planet's inner workings help us in our everyday adventures?

Compass needles don't just point horizontally; they also dip vertically towards the magnetic poles. This dipping effect is minimal at the equator but increases as you move towards the poles. In high latitudes, near the poles, standard compasses can become unreliable without special balancing.

THE CARDINAL DIRECTIONS

Imagine you're standing in the middle of a huge treasure map, and you have to find your way to the hidden treasure. How would you know which way to go? Here's where the cardinal directions come into play! North, South, East, and West—these are the four main points that help everyone from sailors and pilots to hikers and kids in parks navigate the world around them.

These directions are more than just names; they are key tools that help us describe where things are and where we're going. Whether you're planning an epic journey across continents or just trying to find your way to a friend's house, understanding the cardinal directions is your first step in mastering the art of navigation.

They are:

- **North (N):** Is the direction indicated by the red part of all compasses and it points towards the North Pole. It's a special starting point for all other directions.

- **East (E):** Is to the right of north. If you stand facing north and stretch your arms out to your sides, east will be where your right arm points. It's also the direction where the sun rises every day.

- **South (S):** Is the direction opposite to north. If you're facing north, south will be directly behind you.

- **West (W):** Is directly opposite east. Using the same example, if your right arm points to the east, your left arm will point to the west. It's also the direction where the sun sets.

A fun way to remember the order of the cardinal directions is with the phrase: **"Never Eat Soggy Waffles."** This stands for North, East, South, and West, going clockwise around the compass.

WHAT ARE ORDINAL DIRECTIONS

Between the cardinal points, we have ordinal (or intercardinal) directions that help us describe directions that aren't directly north, south, east, or west.

These include:

- **Northeast (NE):** this direction is halfway between north and east.
- **Southeast (SE):** this direction is halfway between south and east.
- **Southwest (SW):** this is halfway between south and west.
- **Northwest (NW):** this is halfway between north and west.

UNDERSTANDING DEGREES

The degrees on a compass help us pinpoint exactly which way we're facing. Think of a compass like a big cake. North, at 0 degrees, is where we make the first cut. As we turn right, or clockwise, the degrees increase until we get all the way around back to north. East is like cutting the cake into four equal parts (90 degrees), south is halfway through the cake (180 degrees), and west is three-quarters of the way (270 degrees). Each direction is precisely measured in degrees so we can follow a very exact path or direction.

Here are the degrees for the ordinal directions:

- **Northeast (NE):** 45 degrees
- **Southeast (SE)** 135 degrees
- **Southwest (SW):** 225 degrees
- **Northwest (NW):** 315 degrees

Understanding these directions is crucial for navigation.

They help you make sense of maps, find places, and even tell others where something is located.

Next time you're out exploring, try to use these directions to describe where things are.

With practice, you'll be a direction expert, ready to lead the way on any adventure!

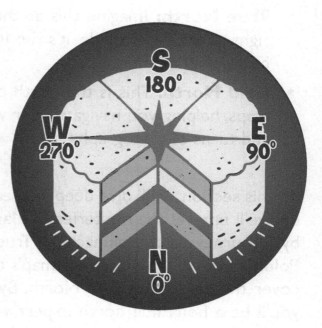

So, remember *"Never Eat Soggy Waffles,"* and use your compass to explore the world confidently.

THE THREE TYPES OF NORTH

Understanding the different types of "north" might seem daunting at first, but fear not! It's actually quite straightforward once you wrap your head around it. There are three key types of north to acquaint yourself with: Magnetic North, True North, and Grid North. Each serves its own purpose and holds its own significance in navigation.

Let's break them down:

- **Magnetic North:** This is the direction your trusty compass needle points towards. It's like your compass's personal GPS, guiding you on your adventures with unwavering accuracy.

- **True North:** Imagine this as the tip-top of the Earth, right at the North Pole. It's the ultimate north, the pinnacle of all directions.
- **Grid North:** This is the north direction you'll find on maps, helping you navigate your way through the twists and turns of cartography.

In this section, we'll dive deep into each type of north. First up, we'll unravel the mysteries of Magnetic North, followed by a journey to the pinnacle of True North at the North Pole. Finally, we'll navigate the map's twists and turns to uncover the secrets of Grid North. By the time we're done, you'll be a bona fide north expert, ready to tackle any navigation challenge with confidence! And stay tuned—later on, we'll show you how to put this knowledge to use and navigate like a pro with your trusty compass!

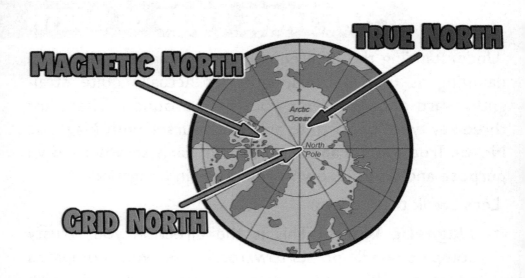

Magnetic North

Magnetic North is like your compass's best buddy—it's the direction that your trusty needle points to. This happens because the compass needle is essentially a tiny magnet itself, and it eagerly aligns with the Earth's magnetic field. Picture the Earth's magnetic field as a colossal invisible force, gently tugging on the magnet in your compass needle, coaxing it to point toward the magnetic north pole.

Now, here's the kicker: the magnetic north pole isn't precisely situated at the geographic North Pole. Nope, it's hanging out in the Arctic, doing its own little magnetic dance. And to keep things interesting, it shifts its position ever so slightly each year due to changes in the Earth's magnetic field.

When you hold your trusty compass flat, the magnetic needle elegantly sways around until it locks onto Magnetic North. This direction is an absolute lifesaver for navigation, providing a reliable reference point no matter where you roam on our planet. But here's the plot twist: Magnetic North and True North (aka the geographic North Pole) aren't always in perfect alignment.

Enter stage left: magnetic declination.

This little nugget of information is the angle between Magnetic North and True North, and it's a real game-changer. You see, this angle varies depending on your location on Earth. In some spots, Magnetic North might cozy up a tad east of True North, while in others, it might lean a smidge west. Knowing the magnetic declination for your neck of the woods is key—it helps you fine-tune your compass readings and navigate like a seasoned pro!

TRUE NORTH

True North, also known as Geographic North, is the direction that points straight towards the North Pole, the unchanging fixed point at the very top of our planet. Unlike Magnetic North, which can shift slightly over time, True North remains constant and is a vital reference in map reading and navigation. The North Pole is where all the lines of longitude meet, making it the ultimate northern point on Earth.

When we talk about True North, we're referring to the direction along the Earth's surface towards the geographic North Pole. This is the direction depicted on most maps, and it's what you would use to navigate when following a map. True North is essential for accurate navigation because it offers a steady, unchanging reference point.

Understanding True North is crucial when using a map and compass together. Most maps are oriented with True North at the top, so knowing how to find True North helps you align your map correctly. For example, if you're in a forest and want to navigate using a map, you would first use your compass to find Magnetic North. Then, you would adjust for the magnetic declination to find True North and align the map so that its top (which represents True North) matches the direction of True North in the real world.

Remember, True North and Magnetic North are not the same. The angle between them is called magnetic declination, and this angle varies depending on your location on Earth. While the compass needle points to Magnetic North, maps are typically aligned to True North. This means you need to adjust your compass readings to account for the difference.

In summary, True North is the direction to the North Pole,

a fixed and unchanging point on the Earth's surface. It serves as the reference point for all geographic and navigational directions. When using a map, aligning it to True North ensures you are correctly oriented and can navigate accurately. Understanding True North helps you bridge the gap between your compass readings and the real world, making it easier to find your way during your adventures.

GRID NORTH

When you look at a map, you'll see lines that run up and down and side to side. These lines help you find places on the map, but they don't always match up with True North or Magnetic North.

Maps, especially topographic maps, use a system called the Universal Transverse Mercator (UTM) or the Military Grid Reference System (MGRS). These systems split the world into squares, making it easier to find and navigate to specific spots. Grid North follows these vertical lines, going from the bottom to the top of the map.

Grid North might be a little different from True North. Generally, the difference between True North and Grid North is only about 2 degrees east or west. For most people, this small difference isn't significant, and it's common to treat Grid North as if it were the same as True North.

So, it's important to know about Grid North, but it's unlikely you'll need such precision to account for the difference between True North and Grid North.

TYPES OF COMPASSES

MAGNETIC COMPASSES: Traditional compasses with a magnetized needle that aligns with Earth's magnetic field, always pointing north.

Simple, reliable, and battery-free, ideal for hiking, camping, and general outdoor navigation.

LIQUID-FILLED COMPASSES: These have a needle suspended in a liquid (usually oil or alcohol), which dampens movement, reducing wobble for steadier readings.

Great for boating, fishing, and uneven terrain.

ELECTRONIC COMPASSES: Digital compasses using sensors to detect Earth's magnetic field, displaying direction electronically.

Found in smartphones and GPS devices, they offer precise, quick readings and features like maps and tracking.

Perfect for advanced navigation and urban exploration.

LENSATIC COMPASSES: Military compasses with a magnifying lens for precise readings while sighting distant objects.

Very accurate for map plotting, ideal for orienteering, land surveying, and military use.

Understanding these compasses helps you choose the right one for activities like hiking with a magnetic compass, boating with a liquid-filled compass, or using an electronic compass on your smartphone.

Alright, young explorer, let's take a closer look at the magnetic compass and discover all its secrets! While it might look simple, a compass is actually crafted with several key parts that work together to guide you on your great adventures. Mastering these components will make navigating with a compass super easy and will turn you into a real navigation expert!

The type of compass we are going to examine is called a baseplate compass, which is an excellent tool for beginners and experts alike. Not only is it inexpensive, often costing less than $10, but it also offers all the essential features needed to navigate effectively. Investing in a baseplate compass from the start is a smart choice as it allows you to harness the full potential of a compass without breaking the bank.

As we explore each part, remember, it's okay if some terms or concepts seem a bit confusing at first. Don't worry—everything will get clearer as we go through the next chapters. We'll take it step by step, ensuring you become confident in using your compass. Ready to start? Let's uncover the secrets of your compass and learn how each piece helps you find your way!

Below, you'll find a handy picture of a compass with all its important bits labeled. Take a good look to get acquainted with each of the components. Then, we'll dive into the nitty-gritty details of what each part does and how you can make the most of them. Ready? Let's go!

The compass shown in the image is a common type; some models might have additional features, while others may have fewer.

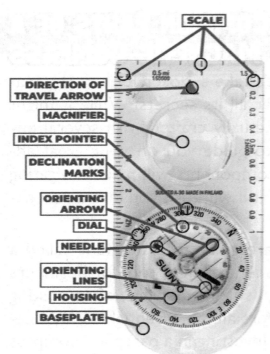

DIRECTION OF TRAVEL ARROW

MAGNIFIER

INDEX POINTER

DECLINATION MARKS

ORIENTING ARROW

DIAL

NEEDLE

ORIENTING LINES

HOUSING

BASEPLATE

SCALE

Baseplate: The baseplate is the foundation of a compass that holds everything together. It is the flat, clear part of the compass, usually made of durable plastic. Its transparency allows you to see through it when placed on a map, helping you align the map with the compass. The baseplate also provides a sturdy surface to hold, ensuring the compass stays steady and points accurately.

Scales: The scales on a compass are the lines and numbers along the edges of the baseplate, like marks on a ruler. They help you measure distances on a map. Each scale corresponds to a specific map type, as different maps have different scales. For example, one map might show that one inch equals one mile. So, if you measure two inches between two points on the map, it means you need to travel two miles in the real world.

By aligning the scale on your compass with the map scale, you can accurately measure distances for your journey. Scales are a crucial tool for connecting the map in your hand to the real world, ensuring you know how far you'll explore.

Direction-of-Travel Arrow: The direction of travel arrow on your compass is a guide pointing you where to go. It's an arrow marked on the baseplate that helps you follow a straight path to your destination. When you're ready to set out, align this arrow with a landmark or a point on your map that you want to head toward.

This arrow helps you walk straight to your target without getting sidetracked. It's like having a friend who always knows the way, pointing you forward and keeping you on track. By using the direction of travel arrow, you can confidently explore and reach your desired spot, knowing you're heading the right way!

Magnifier: On some compasses, you'll find a handy tool called a magnifier. This is a small lens built into the compass, often on the baseplate or attached to swing over the compass face. The magnifier helps you see small details on a map that might be hard to read with just your eyes.

When you're out on an adventure, maps often have tiny symbols, numbers, and lines showing terrain, trails, and landmarks. These details are important for navigating but can be tricky to read. The magnifier makes everything on the map look bigger and clearer, so you can easily see and understand all those small symbols and texts.

Index Pointer: The index pointer, located at the end of the direction of travel arrow, is essential for precise navigation. It sits where the direction of travel arrow meets the edge of the dial (or bezel), marked with degrees. This is where you take degree readings to determine your exact direction.

Housing: The housing of a compass is the shell that protects and holds all the important parts together. It surrounds the compass needle, dial, and other components, keeping everything in place.

The housing is typically made from durable plastic or metal, designed to withstand the elements and any bumps or drops during your adventures. It's transparent on top, allowing you to see all the components clearly.

Needle: The needle of a compass is your trusty guide to the north and one of the most important parts of your compass. This pointer always aims towards the magnetic north.

The needle is a thin piece of magnetized metal that spins freely inside the compass housing. One end, usually painted red, indicates north. This is helpful because, no matter where you turn or how you hold your compass, the red end always points north, helping you determine directions.

By knowing where north is, you can figure out east, west, and south, and navigate effectively.

Dial: The dial, often called the bezel, is a crucial component of a compass. It's a circular ring surrounding the compass needle, usually marked with 360 degrees. Think of it like the face of a clock, but instead of marking hours, it marks directions. Just like on a clock where the numbers 1 through 12 help you tell time, the compass dial has numbers that help you find directions.

The compass dial has written numbers, typically every 20 degrees, with smaller tick marks in between (much like the minute marks on a clock) usually representing 2 degrees each. Each degree on the dial represents a direction relative to North (traditionally marked as 0° or 360°).

The dial allows you to set and follow a precise path by aligning the desired degree mark with the index pointer at the end of the direction of travel arrow. This helps you stay oriented and on track during your journey.

Orienting Arrow: The orienting arrow is an important part of your compass, located inside the compass housing, which turns with the dial. This arrow helps ensure you're following the correct path.

When orienteering, you line up the orienting arrow with the magnetic needle and keep it aligned to maintain your direction. By aligning the orienting arrow with the compass needle, the direction of travel arrow also aligns with your intended direction, ensuring you stay on the right path.

Orienting Lines: Found inside the compass housing alongside the orienting arrow, these parallel lines help you align your compass correctly with a map. They rotate together with the dial and the orienting arrow.

Declination Marks: Declination marks on a compass help you adjust it to point to true north, not just magnetic north. As I explained earlier, the compass needle shows magnetic north, which isn't the exact same spot as true north. Declination marks help you get the direction just right.

Imagine a treasure map—you need to follow directions exactly to find the treasure. Declination marks ensure your compass aligns with your map, so you can navigate accurately.

These marks are useful in places where magnetic north and true north don't line up. Don't worry if this sounds a bit tricky! In the next chapter, I'll show you how to use them.

Mirror: Some compasses come with a built-in mirror, and you might wonder what it's for. The primary function of the mirror in a compass is to help with precision when aligning with a landmark. When you aim your compass at a specific landmark, you can bring the compass to eye level and use the

mirror to see both the compass face and the landmark at the same time. This dual-view allows you to align the compass's direction of travel arrow with the landmark while simultaneously checking that the magnetic needle is properly aligned, ensuring greater accuracy.

Another useful function of a compass mirror is emergency signaling. If you're lost, you can use it to reflect sunlight and flash light in patterns to attract rescuers. This can be a crucial outdoor survival tool.

CHAPTER 3
HOW TO USE A COMPASS

Here we are, finally at the part you've surely been waiting for. We're going to learn how to use a compass!

This chapter will take you step by step through the process, starting with the basics and gradually building up to more advanced techniques.

Using a compass might seem tricky at first, but don't worry—it's all about practice and mastering a few important skills. By the end of this chapter, you'll know how to find north, determine your heading, orient a map to match your surroundings, take a bearing to pinpoint a direction, and follow that bearing to reach your destination.

We'll tackle each skill one at a time, ensuring you have a solid understanding before moving on to the next. Whether you're navigating through a local park, exploring distant trails, or just adventuring in your backyard, these skills will boost your confidence and make you a savvy navigator.

So, let's get ready, grab your compass and possibly a map, and prepare to embark on this journey from beginner to expert navigator. There's a whole world out there waiting for you to explore! Ready to find your way? Let's dive in!

STEP 1: HOLDING THE COMPASS CORRECTLY

Even though it might seem simple, holding a compass correctly is absolutely crucial for it to function properly.

This first step may appear basic, but it sets the foundation for all your compass navigation tasks. If your compass isn't held the right way, it won't give you the accurate information you need to find your way. Let's make sure you start off on the right foot—or hand, in this case!

Ready to learn the proper grip? Let's go!

1. Use a Flat Hand

Start by laying your compass on a flat hand, making sure that the "direction of travel arrow" points straight ahead, towards where you are looking. Keep your palm level to the ground to ensure that the baseplate is horizontal.

Imagine you're holding a small plate full of water—you don't want it to spill!

This position allows the magnetic needle to swing freely and settle pointing north without any tilt or obstruction.

2. Position Your Arm Properly

Extend your arm in front of you at a comfortable angle, keeping the compass in front of your chest. Make sure your arm is steady and your hand remains level. Any tilt can cause the compass needle to touch the dome or base, which might give you an incorrect reading.

3. Keep Metal Objects Away

Make sure there are no metal objects nearby, like rings, watches, or even metal zippers, because these can interfere with the magnetic needle and give you wrong directions. Additionally, it's important to maintain a good distance from large metal structures. To ensure your compass is not affected by magnetic interference, try to stay at least 150 feet away from power lines, 50 feet from cars, and 30 feet from electrified fences for animals.

4. Hold the Compass Steady

When reading your compass, it's important to stand still. Moving around can make the needle swing and give you a wrong direction. Let the needle settle and stop moving before deciding your direction.

5. Double Check

Periodically, gently tap the compass with your free hand while observing the needle. This ensures the needle isn't stuck and is moving freely. Once it settles again, verify the direction to ensure consistent accuracy.

By following these steps, you can hold your compass in a way that maximizes its effectiveness and reliability. Remember, a well-held compass is the first step towards successful navigation.

In this step, we'll learn how to use your compass to find north. This is really important because it helps you make sense of maps, describe where things are, and make smart choices on which paths to take. Let's get started and turn you into a compass wizard!

1. Hold Your Compass Properly:

As explained in Step 1 of this chapter, it's crucial to hold your compass correctly. Make sure it is flat in your hand. This helps the compass needle move freely and gives you accurate directions.

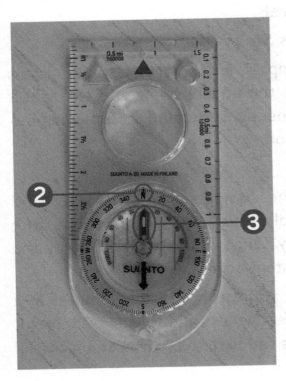

2. Adjust the Dial:

Turn the compass dial (also known as the rotating bezel) so that the 'N' for north on the bezel lines up with the index pointer. This is setting your compass to point to north.

3. Align the Magnetic Needle:

Turn your entire body while holding the compass, using your feet to pivot. Keep the rest of your body steady and don't just twist at the hips or only the compass itself. Rotate until the magnetic needle, often painted red, is contained within the outline of the orienting arrow inside the compass housing.

This step is important to remember whenever you decide to follow a direction. Always remember to align the orienting arrow with the compass's magnetic needle. To help you remember, think of the phrase: "red in the shed."

When the needle is aligned with the orienting arrow, and both are pointing to the 'N' on your bezel, you're facing north.

To Face Other Cardinal Directions:

If you want to change direction, say to face east, simply turn the dial so that the 'E' aligns with the index pointer.

Then, turn your body again until the magnetic needle fits back inside the orienting arrow (red in the shed).

Now, you're facing east.

STEP 3: HOW TO ORIENT A MAP

Orienting a map means setting it up so that north on the map is pointing to the actual north in the real world.

When your map is oriented, you can look from the map to the world around you and understand where things are. If you know where you are on the map, you can look up and see landmarks just like they appear on your map!

Let's dive into how to do this with just a few simple steps.

1. Find a Good Spot:

Lay your map out on a flat, smooth surface. A picnic table, a large rock, or even the ground can work—just make sure you have enough room to see the entire map.

2. Adjust Your Compass:

Turn the compass dial so that north (N) lines up with the index pointer on your compass.

3. Line Up Your Compass with the Map:

Place your compass on the map. The edge of the baseplate of your compass should be parallel to the north-south lines (these are the up-and-down lines) on your map. Make sure the orienting lines and the direction-of-travel arrow on your compass are also parallel with these map lines.

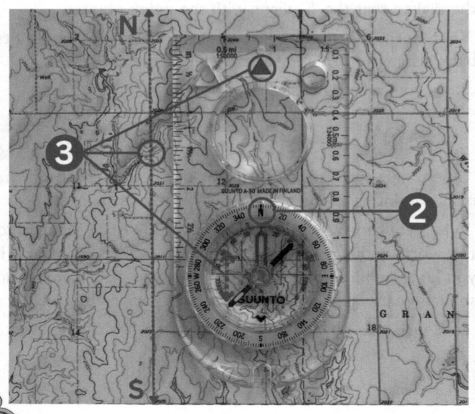

4. Rotate the Map and Compass Together:

Now, turn your map and compass together until the red end of the compass needle is inside the outline of the orienting arrow on your compass (always remember: "Red in the Shed"). Keep everything aligned as you turn.

You Did It!

Now your map is oriented! If you know where you are on the map, you should be able to look around and see the same features in the real world as they appear on your map. This helps you understand your surroundings and navigate better.

STEP 4: TAKING AND FOLLOWING BEARING FROM A MAP

A "bearing" is a super precise way to talk about direction. Instead of just saying "that way" or even "northwest," a bearing uses degrees to show direction. For example, instead of saying 'walk northwest,' you might say 'follow a bearing of 315 degrees.' This means you will walk precisely in the 315-degree direction on the compass, which is more accurate.

Using a bearing ensures you're heading in the exact direction you need to go. Even if two paths start from different places, following the same bearing from each will take you to the same point.

Now that you know the importance of a bearing, let's find and follow one with your compass and map.

I. Line Up Your Compass:

Start by placing your map on a flat surface. Now, grab your compass and put it on the map.

Place the straight edge of the compass baseplate so that it connects your current location on the map (we'll call this "Point A") with the location you want to go to (let's call that "Point B").

2. Point the Arrow:

Make sure the direction of travel arrow on your compass is pointing towards Point B (the place you want to go). This helps you see the direction you'll travel on the map.

3. Align the Compass with Map North:

Carefully rotate the compass bezel (the round part with degrees on it) until the orienting lines inside the compass housing line up with the north-south grid lines on your map. Ensure the north marker on your compass bezel points to north on the map.

4. Read the Bearing:

Now look at the index pointer. The number it points to on the bezel is your bearing. This number tells you the direction you need to follow to get to Point B. In the example of our photo, the direction to follow will be 50 degrees.

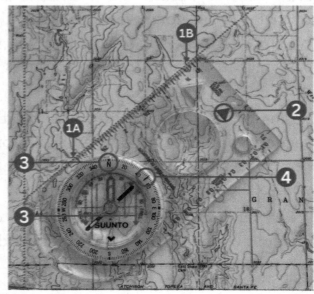

HOW TO USE A COMPASS

FOLLOW THE BEARING

5. Hold Your Compass:

Pick up your compass and hold it so the direction of travel arrow points straight away from you. Be really careful not to twist the bezel while you're holding your compass. If it moves, you might lose your bearing—that's the direction you need to go!

6. Align the Needle (Put red in the shed):

Turn your whole body while holding the compass until the red part of the magnetic needle lines up exactly with the orienting arrow in the compass housing.

7. Follow Your Arrow:

Look where the direction of travel arrow points—that's the way you need to go! But before you start walking, pick a landmark in that direction that isn't too far away. It could be a tree, a big rock, or even a building. Walk towards it, keeping your eye on that spot.

Once you reach your first landmark, choose another one in the same direction and continue towards it. By moving from point to point this way, you'll make sure you're walking straight towards your destination without drifting off course. This is a great way to stay on track as you explore!

Remember, practice makes perfect, so try this out a few times at home with different maps and soon, you'll be a bearing-taking expert ready for any adventure!

STEP 5: TAKING A BEARING IN THE FIELD

Sometimes, your destination isn't always in sight as you walk towards it. It might get hidden behind things like dense forests or hills. By taking a bearing, you can keep heading in the right direction, even if you can't see your endpoint.

1. Spot Your Landmark:

First, pick a land-mark that you want to reach. This could be anything visible in the distance that you want to walk towards.

For even greater accuracy, it's a good idea to hold the compass at eye level. This way, you can aim directly at your target, much like lo-oking through a camera lens. Compasses with a mirror are especially good for this because you can use the mirror to see both the com-pass dial and your landmark at the same time, ensuring you're lined up perfectly. This helps a lot in keeping your direction true as you move towards your adventure!

2. Point Towards Your Landmark:

Hold your compass flat in front of you, making sure it's level. Then, turn your whole body while holding the compass, so the direction of travel arrow points straight at your chosen landmark.

3. Align the Compass (Put red in the shed):

With the direction of travel arrow still pointing towards your landmark, it's time to adjust the compass bezel. Carefully rotate the bezel until the red end of the compass needle sits right inside the outline of the orienting arrow.

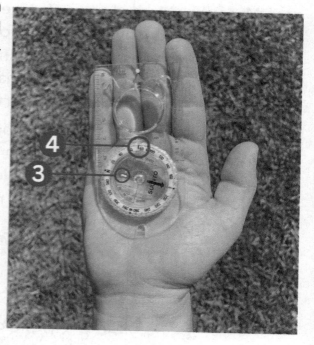

4. Read Your Bearing:

Look at the index pointer. The number you read on the bezel is your bearing. This is the direction you'll follow to get to your landmark.

5. Follow Your Bearing:

To keep going in the right direction, just hold your compass flat and make sure the red needle stays aligned with the orienting arrow as you walk. Keep your eyes on the landscape and your compass, and you'll reach your landmark even if you can't see it the whole time.

STEP 6: ADJUST FOR DECLINATION

Adjusting for declination is a crucial step in compass navigation, especially if you want to align your compass accurately with true north, not just magnetic north. This adjustment is essential for precise navigation and is particularly important when you're using a map alongside your compass. Maps are oriented towards true north, while your compass points to magnetic north. To ensure that both your map and compass are aligned and "speaking the same language," you must adjust for declination so that they are both oriented towards the same north.

Declination is the angle difference between Magnetic North and True North, and it's given in degrees east or west. East Declination means Magnetic North is to the right of True North, while West Declination means Magnetic North is to the left of True North.

Since declination can vary a lot across different parts of the country, it's really important to adjust your compass so you won't end up a quarter-mile away from your destination!

In the continental U.S., declination can vary quite a bit—from nearly 20 degrees east on parts of the West Coast to about 20 degrees west on the East Coast.

IMPORTANT NOTE FOR YOUNG ADVENTURERS:

If you're just starting out with a compass, like making small trips around the park or going on weekend advetures, you might not need to worry about declination right away. For short, everyday explorations where getting slightly off track isn't a big deal, you can keep it simple and just follow the compass needle.

However, as you get more into exploring new places, especially over larger distances or when using detailed maps, knowing how to adjust for declination becomes very important. It ensures that your navigation is accurate, helping you reach your exact destination without unnecessary detours.

Remember, understanding declination is like adding a secret superpower to your compass skills essential for big adventures but not always needed for a fun day out. So, start simple and enjoy your journeys, knowing you can always learn and master this skill as you grow more adventurous!

Imagine going on a mile-long hike and ending up a quarter-mile off your intended path just because of not adjusting your compass—that's why getting this setting right is crucial!

First, you need to find out the declination value for the area you're going to explore. Declination changes depending on where you are on the globe and can even shift over time.

You can find this information on topographic maps (it's usually listed in the legend), but because the Earth's magnetic field slowly changes, these values might get outdated. A super helpful resource is the National Oceanic and Atmospheric Administration (NOAA) website. It has the most up-to-date declination data.

Now let's learn how to set the declination based on your type of compass!

COMPASSES WITH ADJUSTABLE DECLINATION

Compasses with adjustable declination allow you to set the declination semi-permanently, meaning you only need to modify it if you move to an area with a different declination or if several years have passed since the last adjustment.

Different brands of compasses have different systems for adjusting declination, so we'll look at how to adjust it on two popular brands:

- **Brunton Compasses:** These are designed with a tool-free adjustment feature. That means you don't need any special tools to set the declination.

- **Suunto Compasses:** These usually require a small metal key for adjustment. This key is often attached to the compass lanyard, so it's always handy when you need it.

How to Adjust a Brunton Compass

1. Start by holding your compass flat in your hand. Place your thumb on the center hub of the compass and your forefinger on the opposite side of the bottom.

2. With your other hand, hold the outer bezel (the ring with the degrees on it) still. Now, twist the center hub with your pinched fingers. Keep twisting until the declination indicator inside the bezel lines up with your local declination value. This aligns your compass to point to true north without needing any tools.

How to Adjust a Suunto Compass

1. First, find the small metal key. It's usually hanging on the lanyard of your compass.

2. Flip your compass over to find the adjustment screw on the back. Insert the key into this screw. Turn it gently until the declination indicator inside the compass lines up with your local declination value.

Important Reminder: Whenever you're planning a trip, especially to a new area, it's very important to check and reset your compass's declination. Magnetic declination varies from one place to another and can change over time. Adjusting your compass according to the local declination ensures that your navigation is accurate, keeping you on the right path during your adventures.

COMPASS WITH ONLY DECLINATION SCALE

What if your compass doesn't have a special knob or screw to change the declination?

Many compasses come with a declination scale marked inside the compass housing that can help you out. Unlike the previous compasses with semi-permanent declination adjustments, these compasses require you to adjust the declination each time you take a reading.

When adjusting for declination, note the differences between transferring a bearing from the map to the field and vice versa. Let's explore these differences:

From Map to Field:

Let's say you have just taken a bearing from the map and now need to follow it in the field.

1. Suppose the direction you need to follow is 180° (south) and you have a declination of 20 degrees east.

2. Rotate the entire compass and your body until the red magnetic needle points to 20 degrees east on the fixed declination mark inside the compass housing.

3. Now, put red in the shed. Turn the compass bezel (the round part with degrees marked on it) until the orienting arrow is directly over the magnetic needle.

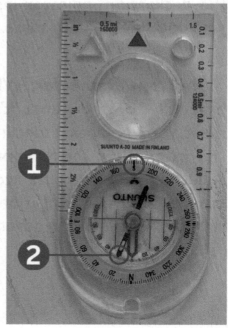

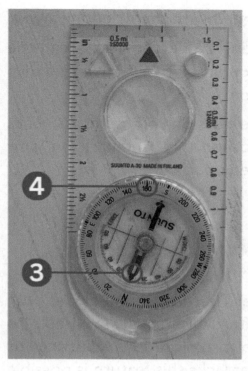

4. The direction that now lines up with the direction of travel arrow and the index pointer shows you the adjusted bearing you need to follow. As you can see from the picture, instead of 180 degrees, the direction will be 160 degrees because of the adjustment of 20 degrees to the east.

From Field to Map:

As in the previous example, let's assume the magnetic declination is 20 degrees east. We've taken a field bearing and now want to transfer it to the map. Let's see how to do it, but here's a secret: forget our mantra "put red in the shed.".

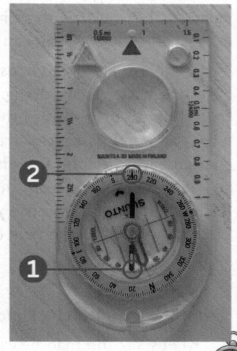

1. Normally, after pointing the direction of travel arrow at your landmark, you would turn the bezel so that the orienting arrow aligns with the magnetic needle. Instead, to account for the 20 degrees east declination, you need to turn the bezel so that the red magnetic needle points to 20 degrees east on the declination scale, which means it will not be aligned with the orienting arrow.

2. With the needle pointing 20 degrees east, read the degrees indicated by the index pointer. This is your true map bearing, adjusted for declination.

For example, if it reads 170 degrees on your compass, that's the bearing you would use to find that landmark on your map, accounting for the magnetic declination.

COMPASS WITHOUT DECLINATION ADJUSTMENT OR SCALE

What if your compass doesn't have declination adjustment features or a declination scale? These days, compasses with declination marks are very affordable, and it's advisable to get one if you're serious about exploration. Adjusting for declination with a compass that lacks this feature is possible but can be tricky, as it's easy to make mistakes with the calculations. However, with a bit of extra knowledge and some manual adjustments, you can still navigate effectively.

Again, there are differences in how we adjust declination based on what we are doing. When navigating from the map to the field, you subtract the declination for east because magnetic north is east of true north. This means your magnetic bearing will be less than your true bearing. Conversely, when navigating from the field to the map, you add the declination for east because you are correcting your magnetic bearing back to the true bearing. Let's see it better with some examples.

From the Map to the Field:

• Let's say the map bearing is 100 degrees and the ma-

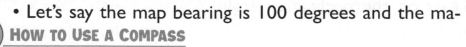

gnetic declination is 10 degrees east. Since the declination is east, subtract the declination number from your map bearing: 100 degrees - 10 degrees = 90 degrees. Your magnetic bearing to follow in the field is 90 degrees.

• If the declination is west, add the declination number to your map bearing. For example, if the map bearing is 100 degrees and the declination is 10 degrees west, add the declination number to your map bearing: 100 degrees + 10 degrees = 110 degrees. Your magnetic bearing to follow in the field is 110 degrees.

From the Field to the Map:

• If your field bearing is 270 degrees and the magnetic declination is 15 degrees east, add the declination number to your field bearing: 270 degrees + 15 degrees = 285 degrees. The true bearing to plot on your map is 285 degrees.

• If the declination is west, subtract the declination number from your field bearing. For example, if the field bearing is 270 degrees and the declination is 15 degrees west, subtract the declination number from your field bearing: 270 degrees - 15 degrees = 255 degrees. The true bearing to plot on your map is 255 degrees.

CHAPTER 4

ORIENTING YOURSELF WITH NATURE

Imagine you're on an adventure in the great outdoors, but you've left your trusty compass behind. Don't worry! Nature is filled with clues to help guide you. While these natural signs aren't as precise as a compass, they still provide valuable insights into your direction.

Navigating using the natural environment is an ancient art. Before compasses and maps, explorers relied on the sun, stars, wind patterns, and even tree shapes to find their way. By learning a few these natural navigation methods, you can become more observant of the natural world and improve your orientation skills, which is especially useful during outdoor adventures or emergencies.

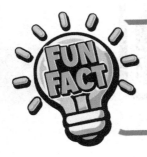

In some regions, ants build their mounds with a slant toward the south to maximize sun exposure, helping keep their mounds warmer. Observing the angle of ant mounds can provide clues about direction.

In the morning, our bright friend rises in the east—so that's where east is. As the day turns into afternoon, the sun heads towards the west to say goodbye. That's how you can find west! But wait, what about north and south? Once you know where east and west are, you can figure those out too. During midday, when the sun is high up, it can be tricky to see where it's moving.

You might have to pay extra attention!

1. Find Your Sunny Spot!

Let's find a place where the sun shines brightly, without any trees or buildings making shadows. A nice flat spot is perfect. If you can choose between grass and a bare patch of dirt, go for the dirt. It's easier to see shadows clearly there!

2. Stick It Out!

Grab a stick, about as tall as a kitchen counter. Plant it right in the ground so it stands up all by itself. Next, find a rock or a small stick and put it right where the end of the shadow touches the ground. This is your first shadow marker. Wait for about half an hour before moving to the next step.

3. Shadow Play!

After waiting (about the time it takes to watch a TV show), come back and see where the stick's shadow is now. It's moved! Mark the new tip of the shadow with another rock. If you have time, wait another while and mark it again. More marks make it easier to tell directions accurately.

4. Connect the Dots!

Now, draw a line on the ground from the first rock to the

last rock using a stick. This line stretches from west to east. To find north and south, draw another line with your stick, going straight across the middle of your west-east line. If you stand with your left foot on the first rock and your right foot on the last rock, you're facing north!

And there you have it, you've just used the sun to find your way! Isn't that cool? Now you can explore and never worry about getting lost as long as you have some sunshine and a stick!

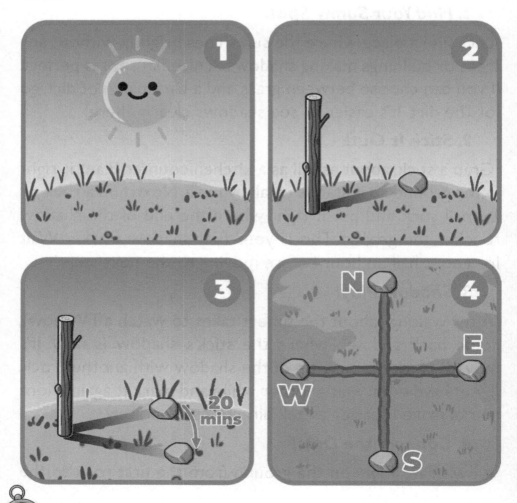

ORIENTING YOURSELF WITH NATURE

When it's dark, go outside and look up to find the North Star, also known as Polaris. It's in the handle of the Little Dipper, a tiny group of stars that looks like a little spoon in the sky. Polaris is special because it always points north. If you can spot it, you're facing north!

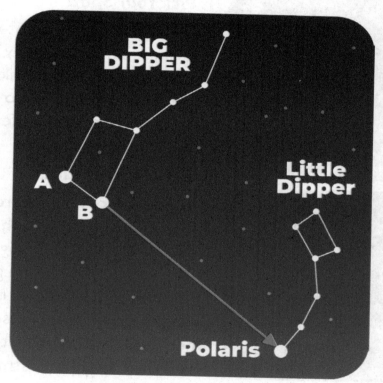

If you can't find the Little Dipper right away, look for the Big Dipper first—it looks like a big ladle or spoon. At the far edge of the Big Dipper's cup, find the two stars that are opposite the handle. These are the pointer stars. Imagine drawing a line starting from the bottom of the cup (B), going through the star at the top (A), and extend that line five times the distance between the pointer stars. The bright star you see on that line is Polaris, the North Star.

Can't Find Polaris? Grab Two Sticks!

Grab two sticks—one a little longer than the other. Even if Polaris hides from you tonight, you can still find your way. Use these sticks to line up any star above you. This way, you can figure out which direction you're facing just by watching the stars. Isn't that cool?

1. Pick Your Spot!

Choose a flat, open spot where you can see the sky clearly. This is your star-gazing stage. Make sure there's enough room to stand and place your sticks a few feet apart.

2. Set Up Your Sticks!

Place the sticks in the ground a few feet apart from each other, making sure they're straight. Stick the shorter one in the ground first, then pick a star in the sky. Put the taller stick in so that, when you line up the tops of both sticks, they point straight to the star.

3. Check the Stars Again!

Wait about 15 or 20 minutes (maybe plan a quick star-gazing game while you wait), then check your sticks and the star again. If the star has moved:

- To the left, you're facing north.
- To the right, you're facing south.
- Upward, you're looking east.
- Downward, you're looking west.

If the star has moved in a mix of directions, like up and to the right, that tells you you're facing southeast. Just think about where the star moved the most to guess your direction!

There you go, young explorers! With these steps, you can use the stars to find your way through the night. Isn't the sky amazing?

NATURE'S CLUES

Although not the most accurate method, nature's hints can provide valuable insights and help verify your direction. The natural world is full of subtle signs if you know what to look for. Observing plant growth patterns, moss on trees, and branch distribution can offer clues. While not always precise, these signs add fun and engagement to your outdoor adventures, helping you connect with the environment and sharpen your observation skills. Let's dive into how you can use these natural indicators to enhance your navigation skills.

Plants and trees love the sun!

Since the sun spends a lot of time in the southern part of the sky (in the northern hemisphere), trees often have more branches and might lean a bit toward the south. If you're exploring in the southern hemisphere, it's just the opposite; trees might lean toward the north.

Moss is another clue!

It usually grows on the north side of trees and rocks in the northern hemisphere because that side is shadier. Take a look at trees and see which side has fewer branches and leaves; that side is probably facing north. If the tree has fruit, check where the fruit ripens quickest—usually on the south-facing side, thanks to the extra sunshine.

In the southern hemisphere, things flip around! Moss tends to grow on the south side because it's shadier there, and trees have denser branches on the north side.

Remember, using nature as your guide isn't always foolproof. Lots of things can affect how plants grow, like how much shade there is. So, use this method as a fun extra check, but not your main way to find direction!

CHAPTER 5

FUN PRATICE EXCERCISES

Are you ready to test your compass skills with some exciting challenges? In this chapter, we'll apply everything you've learned to real-world scenarios, whether in the great outdoors or your backyard.

Think of this chapter as your guide to becoming a true navigator. We'll start with simple exercises to solidify your understanding and then progress to more challenging tasks to sharpen your skills.

Each activity is designed to gradually build your skills, making you proficient with a compass and a master of your own adventures.

And remember, if an activity puzzles you, don't hesitate to ask an adult for help. They can provide guidance and support as you navigate these exciting challenges.

So, put on your explorer's hat, lace up your shoes, and grab your compass—it's time for fun and discovery!

1. CREATE YOUR HOMEMADE COMPASS

Did you know you can make your own compass at home with just a few simple items? This fun activity will not only show you the magic of magnetism but also help you understand how a compass points north.

WHAT YOU'LL NEED

- A needle or straight pin
- A small magnet (refrigerator magnets for examples)
- A small piece of cork or foam
- A shallow dish or bowl
- Water

1. Magnetize the Needle: Hold your needle or pin, and stroke it with your magnet about 30-50 times in one direction. This aligns the tiny magnetic particles in the needle, turning it into a mini magnet itself!

2. Prepare the Floating Base: Cut a small circle or square about the size of a quarter from your cork or foam. This will be the base that helps your needle float.

3. Attach the Needle: Carefully push the magnetized needle through the piece of cork or foam so that it balances and can spin freely. Make sure that half of

the needle sticks out on either side of the cork.

4. Fill Your Dish: Fill your shallow dish or bowl with water. You don't need a lot—just enough to allow the cork and needle to float without touching the bottom.

5. Float Your Compass: Gently place your cork and needle on the surface of the water in the dish. Make sure to place it gently to avoid getting splashed!

6. Watch It Work: Watch as the needle slowly turns and eventually settles pointing north-south. It's finding the Earth's magnetic field just like a real compass!

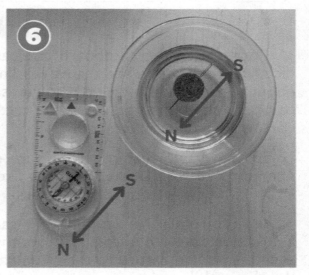

Congratulations, you've just made your very own compass!

Try making your compass in different settings. Does it act the same in every room of your house? What happens if you take it outside?

2. RELAY GAME

This game combines physical activity with learning, as players rush to accurately identify compass points under the pressure of a relay race. It encourages teamwork, quick thinking, and navigation skills.

WHAT YOU'LL NEED

- Two large cardboard compasses with cardinal and ordinal directions clearly marked, including North.
- Real compasses for setting the direction of North accurately.
- Small markers (like cones or stones) for each team.
- Sufficient space to lay out the compasses and for teams to line up at a distance.

HOW TO PLAY:

1. Place each large cardboard compass on the floor at a set distance from where the teams will line up. Make sure there is enough space for the children to run safely. Use a real compass to orient the North point on the cardboard compasses in the correct geographical direction.

2. Split into two teams, making sure each team has the same number of players. Line up in a row like you're getting ready for a race, a bit away from your compass.

3. Listen carefully! An adult or your game leader will shout out a direction like "Northeast" or "Southwest". The first player in each team's line dashes to their compass and puts a marker on the shouted direction.

4. If you get it right and place your marker on the exact spot, go stand behind the compass, facing your team to show you're done. If it's not quite right, no worries! Just run back to your line, and you'll get another chance when it's your turn again.

5. Keep going! The next player in line will wait for a new direction and then it's their turn to run. The game ends when every player on one team has correctly placed their marker and is standing behind their compass. That team wins!

This game is super flexible! You can play it anywhere, from your backyard to a park, or even in your room, as long as you have your trusty compass.

WHAT YOU'LL NEED

- A compass for each player
- A piece of paper to keep score

HOW TO PLAY:

1. One player starts by looking around to find something interesting like a bird in a tree, a stuffed animal, or even a funny book on a desk.

2. Check the compass to see which direction the object is in. Is it South? North-East? Or another direction?

3. Based on what you see, come up with a fun question for the other player. For example, if you spot a bird in a tree to the south, you could ask, "Can you find something that flies and sings in the south direction?" Or, if you see a comic book on a desk to the north-east, ask, "Can you see something fun to read in the north-east direction?"

4. The other player then uses their compass to guess which object you're talking about. If they guess right, they earn a point!

5. Now it's the other player's turn to look around, use the compass, and ask a question.

Keep playing until you decide to stop. The player with the most points wins!

4. COMPASS BINGO

Compass Bingo is a creative twist on classic bingo, using compass directions to guide you in filling out your bingo card! This game not only adds an artistic element as you draw items in designated squares but also helps you learn compass directions. It's fun, engaging, and educational—perfect for mastering your navigation skills!

WHAT YOU'LL NEED

- A bingo card for each player, with 16 or 25 squares
- Pens or pencils for drawing
- A master card for the leader with pre-drawn items
- A list of compass directions (cardinal and optionally ordinal directions) displayed on each player's card

HOW TO PLAY:

1. Each player receives a bingo card with empty squares. At the top or bottom of the card, the 4 (or 8) cardinal points could be marked to make it easier for those who are beginners.

2. The leader has a master card with different items drawn in various squares. The leader will use compass directions to describe which square the players should work on.

3. The leader picks a square and describes its location using compass points. For example: "Find the northmost square, then move as far west as you can. Draw an 'A' there." Players follow these directions and draw the specified item in the correct square.

4. Continue giving directions for each item. The leader marks off each called item on the master card to avoid repetition. For younger players, provide occasional hints, like "the next square is right next to the tree you just drew."

5. The game continues until all squares on each player's card are filled. Players can then share and compare their drawings with each other.

You and your friends will team up, throw a beanbag in different directions, and race to find it using your compass skills. "Compass Toss" is perfect for a sunny day in the park. It's all about teamwork, direction, and lots of laughs!

WHAT YOU'LL NEED

- A compass for each team
- A beanbag for each team

HOW TO PLAY:

1. Gather your friends and form teams. Each team should have at least four players.

2. Each player in the team gets their own direction: North, South, East, or West. If you have more players, you can use additional compass directions like Northwest (NW) or East-Southeast (ESE).

3. The first player sets their compass to their assigned direction and faces that way. Holding the beanbag, this player throws it as far as they can in the direction they are facing.

4. Once the beanbag lands, the rest of the team races to find where it fell. The second player then goes to where the beanbag landed, sets their compass for their direction, and throws the beanbag again.

5. The game continues with each team member taking turns. Each time, set the compass, face the right direction, and toss the beanbag. Remember to follow your directions closely!

6. You can set a time limit or a number of rounds after which the game ends. The fun is in playing and enjoying, not just winning!

6. CLOSED COURSE CHALLENGE

One person or one team will create a course by giving directions that start and finish at the same spot. They'll write these directions on a piece of paper. The other person or team will follow these directions using a compass. If done correctly, they will complete the loop and return to the starting point. It's a great way to practice your compass skills and have a lot of fun at the same time!

WHAT YOU'LL NEED

- A compass
- A marker like a beanbag or a small flag
- A notebook to jot down directions

HOW TO PLAY:

1. Choose Your Playground: This game is best played in a big open area like a schoolyard or a park.

2. Mark Your Territory: Each team starts by placing their marker at their starting point.

3. Create Your Course: Each participant or team will create a path starting from the marked point. For every move, write down the number of steps taken and the direction (either cardinal direction or bearing). Make sure that your path loops back to the starting point.

4. Exchange Directions: Once each team has created their course, exchange the lists of directions with another team or participant.

5. Follow the Compass: Teams will then use their compass to follow the set of directions provided by another team. The challenge is to navigate accurately to ensure you end up back at your starting marker.

EXAMPLE COURSES:

Simple Loop (Using Cardinal Directions)

1. Walk 5 paces North.

2. Walk 5 paces Est.

3. Walk 3 paces South.

4. Walk 10 paces West.

5. Walk 2 paces South.

6. Walk 5 paces Est.

More Complex Loop (Using Specific Bearings)

1. Take a bearing of 270 degrees and walk 20 paces.

2. Take a bearing of 45 degrees and walk 25 paces.

3. Take a bearing of 135 degrees and walk 30 paces.

4. Take a bearing of 225 degrees and walk 26 paces.

5. Take a bearing of 0 degrees and walk 22 paces.

The key to success in the Closed Course game is accurate pacing and correct use of the compass. It's a fantastic way to see how well you can navigate and a great game for sparking a sense of adventure!

7. GEOMETRIC SHAPES

This exciting outdoor game will teach you how to use a compass to create geometric shapes. Follow specific compass directions to walk a hidden path that forms a shape, like a square or triangle.

WHAT YOU'LL NEED

- A compass for each player or for every pair of players
- Wrapped candies to use as markers and prizes
- A spacious outdoor area like a park or a large backyards

HOW TO PLAY:

1. Place the wrapped candies on the ground, spacing them several meters apart. Each candy marks the starting point for a shape.

2. Use your compass to find north. Walk the number of paces in the direction indicated by the game leader. For example, if your first instruction is "5 paces North," make sure you walk straight towards north for 5 paces.

3. Next, you might need to turn to the east and take more steps. The leader will give you all the directions one by one—like "5 paces East," then "5 paces South," and finally "5 paces West."

If you followed all the directions correctly, you should end up right back where you started, next to your candy! You can now collect the candy as your prize.

4. After everyone has made a square, try other shapes! Change the number of paces or directions to make triangles, rectangles, or even a star pattern for a challenge. Increase the number of paces or add more complex shapes as you get better at using your compass.

Directions for the Rectangle: 4 paces north, 8 paces east, 4 paces south, 8 paces west.

Directions for the Square: 5 paces north, 5 paces east, 5 paces south, 5 paces west

8. ANIMAL ADVENTURE

Animal Adventure is a playful and educational game where you'll use a compass and your favorite animal friends to learn about directions! Whether you have a picture of an animal or your beloved stuffed animal, this game will help you understand compass points in a fun and interactive way. It's all about placing your animal in the right direction and then navigating them to new spots based on compass bearings.

WHAT YOU'LL NEED

- A picture of an animal for each player, or a favourite stuffed animal
- A large cardboard cutout with the letter "N" for North

HOW TO PLAY:

1. Use a compass to find north in your play area. Tape the cardboard "N" to the wall or the floor to mark North clearly for everyone.

2. The leader will call out directions for where each animal should be placed. For example, the leader might say, "Will the Tiger please sit at northeast?" Each player places their animal at the directed compass point relative to North.

3. Once all animals are in place, the game becomes more interactive. Players can suggest new movements for their animals. For instance, a player might say, "Tiger, where are you and where would you like to go?" The player might answer, "I'm down south and I would like to go northest."

4. Since only North is marked, players must figure out where the other compass points are located based on their understanding of direction. Move the animals according to the new directions called out.

5. The game can continue with players moving their animals around different compass points until everyone has had a turn or you can set a time limit.

9. HIDDEN SHAPES

This game is perfect for young adventurers like you, especially if you're just starting to learn how to use a compass. Set in a large outdoor area, such as a campsite or park, this treasure hunt will have you navigating to find hidden treasures attached to trees and bushes.

Consider having an adult leader accompany each team to help with directions and ensure safety.

WHAT YOU'LL NEED

- Construction paper cut into shapes of flowers or animals.
- Pushpins to securely attach your shapes to trees or bushes.
- A large outdoor space with accessible trees or bushes.
- A set of written directions for each team that will guide them to their designated target.

HOW TO PLAY:

1. An adult will prepare the game area by attaching the paper shapes of flowers or animals to various trees or bushes with pushpins. Ensure that each shape is visible and securely fastened.

2. Organize into small teams—each group will act as a team of explorers. Distribute a unique set of written directions to each team.

3. All teams start from the same point. When the game begins, follow your team's directions. Your directions might instruct you to go "12 paces East, then 34 paces North." Count each step and follow the compass directions carefully!

4. Use your directions to lead you to a specific tree or bush where your hidden shape awaits. Once you find your shape, celebrate your successful navigation!

5. After finding the first shape, teams can exchange their sets of directions with each other and search for new treasures. Continue the adventure by following new trails.

You and your friends will make up your own paths by writing down each twist and turn, and then you'll see if you can follow each other's trails. You can play this game anywhere— in a park, in your backyard, or even during a camping trip. If you're super brave, try playing it at night with flashlights to add an extra layer of adventure!

WHAT YOU'LL NEED

- A compassPen and paper (to write down your adventure path)
- Two Popsicle sticks per team (these are your trail markers)
- Flashlights (if you're brave enough to play in the dark!)

HOW TO PLAY:

Getting Ready:

1. Form Your Teams: Gather up into small groups, called patrols. Each group should have about 3-5 friends.

2. Grab Your Gear: Each patrol gets a compass, a piece of paper, a pen, and two Popsicle sticks.

3. Place Your Starting Marker: Put one of your Popsicle sticks in the ground where you'll start your trail. This is your trail's "home base."

Let's Make a Trail!

1. Create Your Path: Decide where you want to go and use your compass to find out which way to walk. Write down each part of your path on the paper, like "walk 25 steps North" or "go 10 steps Northwest." Think of fun and tricky ways to make your trail interesting!

2. End Your Trail: When you get to the end of your trail, put down your second Popsicle stick. This tells everyone, "The trail stops here!"

3. Trade Trails: Swap your trail directions with another patrol. Start at the Popsicle stick of another team's trail and use their directions to find the end.

11. COMPASS GOLF

In Compass Golf, you'll aim to hit a golf ball into a buried tin can at the center of a circle. Marked with North, South, East, and West points, you'll test your aiming skills from each direction. Count your strokes and see who can sink the ball with the fewest hits.

WHAT YOU'LL NEED

- A small tin can
- A large circle marked on the ground
- Small pegs to mark the North, South, East, and West points on the circle's circumference
- A golf ball and club for each player

HOW TO PLAY:

1. Bury the small tin can in the center of a large circle that you've marked on the ground. This can will be the target for your golf shots.

2. Place small pegs at the North, South, East, and West points along the circumference of the circle. These marks will be your starting points, or "tees," from where you'll take your golf shots toward the can in the center.

3. Each player takes turns at each directional peg (North, South, East, and West). The goal is to hit the golf ball into the tin can from these points.

4. Record how many strokes each player needs to get the ball into the can from each directional tee. Fewer strokes are better!

5. After taking a shot from one direction, move to the next peg in the sequence (for example, from North to East), and take your next shot. Continue until each player has shot from all four directions.

6. After all players have taken shots from all four points, tally the strokes each player used to sink the ball into the can from each direction. The player with the fewest total strokes wins.

Are you ready to put your compass skills to the test and have loads of fun with your friends? Let's play a game called CompassBall. It's like basketball but with a twist—you'll use your knowledge of directions to score points!

WHAT YOU'LL NEED

- A basketball
- A basketball court
- Some cones or sidewalk chalk (to mark spots on the court)

HOW TO PLAY:

1. On the basketball court, use the cones or chalk to mark 8 spots. These spots are secret because they stand for directions like North, South, East, and West, and the ones in between like Northeast. Remember, don't write which spot is which because finding them is part of the game!

2. Split into two teams. Each team will take turns to play.

3. Listen for the Direction: At the start of your turn, an adult, a referee, or the captain of a team will call out a direction, like "North" or "Southeast."

4. Quickly think and run to the spot on the court that matches the direction called out.

5. If you're at the correct spot, you get 2 points and can shoot the basketball to try and score a basket. If you make the basket, you earn an extra point! But, if you're at the wrong spot, you miss your chance to shoot this turn.

6. Everyone gets a chance to run, think, and shoot! We'll keep going until everyone has had the same number of turns.

7. At the end, we add up all the points. The team with the most points wins the game!

13. PASSWORD HUNT

In the Password Hunt, teams race to find hidden password pieces and be the first to assemble their password!

WHAT YOU'LL NEED

- **Compass:** *Each team gets a compass to navigate.*
- **Password Pieces:** *Each team's password is cut into three parts and hidden separately.*
- **Starting Point:** *All teams start from the same place.*

HOW TO PLAY:

1. Prepare the Passwords: Write a secret password on a piece of paper for each team. Then cut each password into three pieces. You can make the game even more interesting by using a question or a riddle as the password that teams must answer once they collect all their pieces.

2. Hide the Password Pieces: Choose different places in the game area to hide the password pieces. You can adjust the difficulty of the game from easy (cardinal directions), medium (ordinal directions) to difficult (specific bearing).

3. Mark the Starting Point: All teams start from the same location. This could be a big tree, a bench, or any clear landmark in your playing area.

4. Start the Hunt: Each team lines up at the starting point. When the leader says "Go!" each team uses their compass to find the first piece of their password. Follow the compass to find each password piece, with challenges or extra clues adding excitement!

6. Collect All Pieces: Once you find a piece, figure out the next direction to find the next one. Keep track of each piece as you collect them.

7. Race to the Finish: After finding all the pieces, hurry back to the start. The first team with their complete password or the correct answer wins!

"Penny Pathfinder" is a thrilling navigation game that uses a compass and a bit of geometry to bring you back to where you started! By following bearings and counting your steps, you'll create a triangle and try to end up exactly where you began. This game is perfect for sharpening your compass skills and understanding how angles work in real life.

WHAT YOU'LL NEED

- A penny
- A compass
- Open space suitable for walking

HOW TO PLAY:

1, Start by placing a penny on the ground right at your feet.

2. Set your compass to any bearing you like (for example, 60 degrees). Take a sighting along that bearing, then walk exactly 10 paces in that direction.

3. Add 120 degrees to your initial bearing. For example, if you started at 60 degrees, your new bearing will be 180 degrees. Take a sighting on this new bearing and walk another 10 paces.

4. Add another 120 degrees to your current bearing and repeat: ake a sighting and walk 10 paces.

5. Add one more set of 120 degrees to your bearing, take a sighting, and walk your final 10 paces.

6. Stop and look down at your feet. If all went well, you should find yourself back at your starting point, right where the penny is!

Practice makes perfect! Don't worry if you don't get it right the first time. Adjust your bearings or your pace count and try again.

15. THE BOX GAME

In this adventure, you'll put on a special box that covers your eyes but lets you see your compass. You'll use the compass to follow directions given by a friend and try to find hidden treasure! The goal of this game is to teach you to rely solely on your compass, without using your sight to orient yourself.

WHAT YOU'LL NEED

- A compass to guide you.
- A navigator box, which we'll make sure you can see your compass through.
- A friend who will give you step-by-step directions to find the treasure.

HOW TO PLAY:

1. Put on your navigator box at the starting line. Check that you can see your compass clearly.

2. Your friend will read out directions like, "Turn East and walk 8 steps," then, "Turn North and walk 10 steps." It's your job to use your compass to find the right direction and then count your steps carefully.

3. Follow the directions accurately, and you'll find yourself right at the treasure! What will it be? Maybe some candy or another cool surprise.

Adults will be around to make sure everyone is safe and having a good time. This is a game of skill and patience, not speed. Focus on following the directions and using your compass correctly.

Are you ready for the ultimate adventure? You've worked your way through simpler activities, and now you're about to tackle the most challenging and exciting one yet—becoming a treasure hunter for the day!

For this exciting adventure, you'll need at least two people. One person will have the important job of hiding the clues and the treasure, as well as creating the instructions to follow in order to find them. This includes writing down the directions and the number of steps for each clue. It's a very important task!

The other person will be the brave explorer who searches for the clues and the treasure. This way, everyone gets to play a part in our treasure hunt.

Through this game you will improve important skills such as taking and following a bearing, estimating distances and solving problems. So grab a partner, get your compass ready, and let's start the journey to uncover hidden treasures!

WHAT YOU'LL NEED

- A compass
- Treasure hunt clues (prepared in advance)
- Small treasures or prizes to hide
- A notebook to jot down your clues and directions
- A friend or family member to join the hunt (optional)

HOW TO PLAY:

Treasure Setup Guide:

1. Choose a Great Spot for Your Hunt: Pick a fun place like your backyard, a park, or even a beach. This is going to be where our treasure map comes to life!

2. Selecting and Hiding the First Clue: Choose a starting point and look around for a clever place to hide the first clue. You could use spots like behind a tree, near a garden statue, or under a park bench. You can make the game more or less challenging depending on where you choose to hide the items. If you want an easier game, pick more obvious spots. For a tougher challenge, be more creative and choose harder-to-find locations.

3. Prepare Your Compass and Take Bearing: Once you have chosen the first hiding spot for the clue, it's time to take a bearing. Here's a quick refresher on how to take a bearing (for more details, see page 38, "Taking a Bearing in the Field"):

- Start by positioning yourself at the starting point of the treasure hunt.

- Hold your compass flat and point the direction of travel arrow at your chosen landmark (the hiding spot for the clue).

- Rotate the bezel until the red end of the compass needle is inside the orienting arrow.

- Read the bearing at the index pointer and record it.

4. Walk to the Hiding Spot and Count Steps: As you walk, count your steps carefully and record it next to the bearing.

Note: if an adult is setting up the treasure hunt, make sure to adjust the step size to match that of a child's steps. This ensures the clues are accurate and easy to follow for the young explorers.

5. Repeat the Process for Subsequent Clues: From the first hiding spot, choose the next location to hide the following clue then repeat step 3 and 4.

6. Set Up More Clues: Repeat the process for each new clue. Find another spot, align your compass, count your steps, and write down the clue.

7. Prepare Clues and Hide Them: Once you have collected all the bearings and step counts, it's time to prepare the clues. Each clue should contain the direction (bearing) and the number of steps needed to find the next hiding spot.

- For each clue, write down the bearing and the number of steps. For example, "Walk 30 steps at 45 degrees to find your next hint."

- To make the game more exciting, you can add minor surprises at each clue location. For instance, hide small treats or toys at each spot. Alternatively, you can include a fun action on each clue card, such as "Do 10 jumps" or "Spin around twice" before moving on to the next clue.

- Go to each hiding spot and place the corresponding clue there. Make sure the clues are well-hidden but still findable by the players.

- Give the players the first clue, which leads to the first hiding spot, at the start of the game.

Guide for the Treasure Hunters:

1. Starting the Treasure Hunt: To begin the treasure hunt, position yourself at the starting point. Take the first clue and read the directions carefully. You will see a degrees (bearing) and the number of steps you need to walk. Turn the bezel until the degrees indicated on the clue aligns with the index pointer on your compass.

2. Put Red in the Shed: Hold the compass flat in your palm and make sure it's level. Turn your whole body while holding the compass until the red part of the magnetic needle lines up exactly with the orienting arrow in the compass housing.

3. Walking to the Clue: At this point, begin walking in the direction indicated by the direction of travel arrow on your compass. Count your steps carefully as specified in the clue. To ensure you stay on course, look for a reference point in the distance that aligns with your direction of travel. By keeping your eyes on this distant reference point, you can maintain a straight path towards your next clue.

4. Discover the Next Clue: Once you have walked the specified number of steps, start looking around the area for the hidden clue. When you find the clue, read it carefully to get the next set of directions and repeat the process.

5. Finding the Treasure: As you follow the clues and get closer to the end of your adventure, you will eventually reach the final clue. This last clue will guide you to the treasure's hiding spot

When you arrive at the final location, search carefully to uncover the hidden treasure. Celebrate your success and enjoy the rewards of your journey.

Start Your Hunt: Begin at a starting point with your compass and the first clue. Use the compass to find the right direction, and count your steps carefully to reach your next clue.

Follow the Clues: Use your compass to navigate from one clue to the next. Each treasure should lead you closer to the final prize. Keep your eyes peeled and your wits about you!

Keep Track of Your Journey: As you follow the clues, write down any landmarks you pass and how the directions change. This will help you stay on track and might even assist you in creating your own treasure hunt in the future.

Find the Final Treasure: The last clue should lead you to a "grand treasure." Celebrate your successful adventure and enjoy your findings!

Great job on completing your Compass Treasure Hunt! Think about different themes or stories you could use to make the clues even more exciting.

BONUS
KIDS ADVENTURE PACK

SCAN ME!

33 Interactive Compass and Map Games: Fun exercises and printable maps to teach kids compass skills, cardinal directions, and spatial awareness.

Engaging Hands-On Activities: Involves cutting, pasting, and coloring to reinforce practical learning through interactive play.

Suitable for All Ages: Designed for children of various age groups to learn at their own pace and enjoy the process.

CONCLUSION

Congratulations, young explorer!

You've reached the end of our journey together through the fascinating world of compasses and navigation. Each chapter was crafted to give you the tools and knowledge to embark on your own real-life adventures.

As you close this book, don't think of it as the end of your learning. Instead, see it as the beginning of your exploration into the great outdoors and beyond. The skills you've acquired here are just the starting point for all the amazing journeys you will take. Remember, a true explorer is always curious, always learning, and always ready for an adventure.

Keep your compass handy and your eyes on the horizon. Use your new skills to find new paths, solve mysteries, and discover the wonders of the world around you. Each step you take into nature is a step filled with potential for discovery and excitement.

So lace up your boots, grab your compass, and step out the door with confidence. You have the tools and the knowledge to chart your own course. Have fun exploring, stay curious, and remember: every great explorer started exactly where you are right now—with a sense of wonder and a desire to discover.

Here's to your adventures, big and small. May your compass always point you in exciting directions, and may you always find your way back home with stories to tell and dreams of your next journey.

Happy exploring, young adventurer! The world is waiting for you.